*Susa*inc

By: Nazila Fathi

Graphic Designer: Kamran Ashtari

First Edition: 2020

Published by Susa Inc

www.Susainc.org

My
Name
Is
Cyrus

In the west, you know me by my Greek name, Cyrus, and in the east, by my Persian name, Kourosh. I am the Great King, the founder of the largest empire of the ancient world. My father was Cambyses, the king of a small kingdom called Persia.

I founded the Persian Empire over 2,500 years ago.

Until then, the Persians lived in the mountains. They were so poor they wore scratchy leather clothes. They had very little food to eat and their children often went to sleep hungry.

And even so, the rulers of the neighboring kingdoms attacked them and looted the little food they had. "Serve your masters," they yelled as they burned down their homes and farms and stole their livestock.

But I knew the Persians deserved better. They were smart and hardworking. These men and women had created a genius work of engineering called *qanat* with the few tools they had. *Qanat* was a system consisting of many deep wells that were connected underground. The canal that connected the wells brought fresh rainwater from under the rocks to the surface. You can still find these *qanats* in some parts of Persia—the country you call Iran now.

As a child, I was trained to be a warrior. When I saw the suffering of my people, I told them it was time to fight for better lives. "You need to stop the bullies," I told them.

"If you want to live better, you must fight for it."

To my surprise, they accepted my leadership. My commanders trained them to fight and taught them to build weapons. They built swords, spears, chariots, bows and arrows.

Other tribes joined us because they were tired of tyranny too. Legend has it that I built the largest army in the world. After many battles, my army and I defeated the tyrants.

Then, I founded the largest empire ever on earth. It stretched to the four corners of the world as we used to say because back then we thought the world was flat.

My children made the empire larger and wealthier. My son, Cambyses II, who was named after my father, conquered Egypt. Egypt had been a great empire with a powerful army.

My daughter, Atoosa, became a powerful empress. She married Darius, one of my commanders who sat on the throne after both my sons died.

Darius made the empire rich. He built roads and introduced law and order in the regions under his rule.

Atoosa lived a long life and was widely respected.

Do you know why people call me Cyrus the Great? No, not because I founded the largest empire on earth.

Not at all!

You see, in the ancient world, when rulers conquered a place, they moved people away from their homes to break up their traditions. They enslaved them and took their children to new places so they forgot their parents' way of life.

People call me Cyrus the Great because wherever I went I respected people's traditions. "Set all the slaves free," I ordered my army when we marched into Babylon, the capital of one of the largest empires I liberated.

I told war prisoners that they were free to live in their homes, the ones they lived in before the fall of the kings, as long as they were honest.

Did you know I liberated the Jews in the city of Babylon where they had been enslaved for 70 years? My name is mentioned 23 times in the Jewish Bible as their liberator.

"Cyrus is just and wise," people told one another.

Babylonians danced and sang in celebration. They called me the Son of God.

Even though I had little gold, I felt I was the richest man on earth because I had the most loyal army and people.

I proclaimed on a piece of clay in the shape of a barrel that all humans must be free to practice their traditions and religions.

The barrel-shaped clay is called the Cyrus Cylinder and is kept at the British Museum in London. It is as small as a ball and you can hold it in your hands.

The Persian Empire became wealthy and prosperous. Iranians live in a small part of that land today but they feel proud to belong to the empire I founded. They refer to me as the Father of the Nation.

And nearly 2,000 years later, the leaders of a new country very far away from Persia—called the United States of America—decided to respect different traditions too. One of their leaders, Thomas Jefferson, studied how I had ruled and decided no single religion can dominate his country.

I lie in a small tomb in southern Iran. The stones to the monument are chipped but the tomb has remained largely intact.

Just recently, a little girl visited me and asked her mother curiously, "Why isn't Cyrus buried under a golden dome?"

"Shouldn't a great leader who conquered so much land have a magnificent tomb?"

Her mother squeezed her hand and said, "Many leaders who were buried under tall pillars and shiny domes have long been forgotten but people have paid their respect to this humble tomb for centuries."

But let me tell you a secret. It gives me great pleasure when people travel long distances to visit a man from the ancient past.

Will you visit me one day?

I will be waiting for you.

QUIZ

When did Cyrus found the Persian Empire?

a. In 2019

b. Yesterday

c. 2,500 years ago

d. 500 years ago

Why was Cyrus called Cyrus the Great?

a. Because he was very tall.

b. Because he was just and fair.

c. Because he was rich.

d. Because he had great hair.

Where is Cyrus buried?

a. In the United Kingdom

b. In the United States

c. In Canada

d. In Iran

How were these people related?

Cyrus	Cyrus's daughter
Atoosa	Atoosa's husband
Cambyses I	Cyrus's father
Cambyses II	or Kourosh
Darius	Cyrus's son

Maze

Help Atoosa find th
Cyrus Cylinder

www.ingramcontent.com/pod-product-compliance
Lightning Source LLC
Chambersburg PA
CBHW060753150426
42811CB00058B/1396